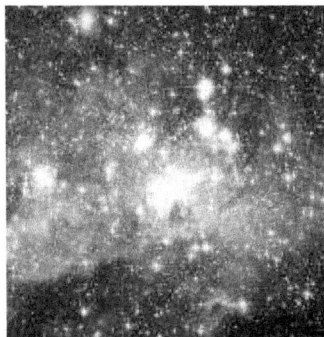

Stars
at
Naught

Owen Patterson

BREVIS Publishing ■ Chicago

Life universally
Converses adversity
Inconspicuously conspicuous
Inspiration

Words crawl
To evolve
Utterances walk
Between chaos and order

Running to see
Falling to learn
Waking to dream
Humility... and perspective
Offer clarity of thought
As do
Stars at Naught

Titles by Owen Patterson

The Dis-condition of Ease (prose fiction, 2015)

Lovely Faze (poetry, 2017)

Stars at Naught (poetry, 2018)

Jaded (poetry, 2018)

Fear Naught
The Junk Drawer of Poetry (poetry/prose, 2019)

See online book reviews at *Windy City Reviews*

BREVIS Publishing, Chicago, IL USA; 2018 **EDIT** x2-2.97
ISBN: 978-0-9964834-4-5 (BREVIS)

Formatting by Owen Patterson
Cover design by "Pica"; Edmund Barca
Editing by Gallus "Giblet" Morsél

Special Thanks:
Yasmeen Patterson Ahmad, Edmund Barca Gaylord,
Gallus Morsél, Larry Nance, Sarah Yu

Thanks for your advice and help.

Karin Janine

We Are Twine

I Remember
So Not To Be Forgotten

CONTENTS

CONTENTS

It is but a match lit
Held in the palm
Fire
Born of heart and soul
When extinguished
At that moment
Reborn
A giant corona
Exploding
In a black universe

The Match Lit Corona

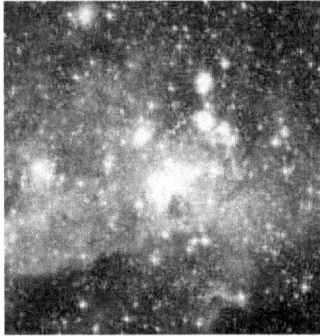

Stars

To converse adversity is to overcome

Wake, to overcome endless sleep
Eat, to overcome hunger
Walk, to overcome stagnation

The first breath, overcomes the Naught
The last, overcomes All

Life Adverse

Gaze
The naught sky
Light-filled eyes
Can see again
The bleak
Washed away

Stars at Naught

Block Writer's

Blocked…

Deepest black
Pins emerge
Lights swirl
Mingle
Rudimentary elements
Stumbling
Grand Petri Dish
Coalesces singularity
Vantage
Painful and blinding
Leading to
Crackle and pop
Charged constructs
Potential
Static
EXPLOSION!
Here we are

Now write…

Buckin' Star

Enter the buck that stars
Enter and see
Constellation and queen

Says Pass-er Buy-er
"Excuse me. Excuse me. Excuse me!"
To Stand-er There-er Transfix-er Buy-er
Transfixin' luminous wreck-tangle
Crook neck-tangle
Bad posture in the way

Contact not eye
Melancholy soundtrack
Plays high
Cool folks
And laptops
And smartphones
And tech manuals
And coffee cups
No handles

Giant landscape
Backdrop warm
Cool art
Landfill form
Every space
Save the mind
Cool art embrace
Not unkind
Cool art un-go
Un-notice may
Crook neck-tangle
Bad posture in the way

And smile
And happy
And again

Write...

Self

If only...
To be so serene
So natural
To be self

Freckles Constellāte

Your face
Lovely
Freckles constellāte
Above me
Big scene pictured
Small screen figured
Diminutive
Yet, never abate

Maintain ease
Please
No cover
No base
Your face
Comforts

So, well I comport
For your face
Is lovely
Your freckles, constellāte
Above me

Closed eyes
Thought self a star
Looked into the heavens
Saw a billion billion stars
And was humbled

Continuum
Stars
Open eyes

Six days passed

comas and humility

Contradiction

Good night

Sleep now
The sun will come
To your window
Challenge
Experience
Another day

Awake
Sunlight spills in
Came the sun last night
In dreams
Cleansed eyes
In darkness
Warmed hearts
In the chill of fall
Lifted grime from skin
Collected in days living
Made motions fluent
Even in stillness
In death
In sleep
In dreams

Good morning

Cerebral Retroflex

Rēcognition

Gears turn
Cogs lace
Plates embrace
And unlace
Propel recollection
Collection again
Cerebral retroflection

Redundancies guaranty
That gears and cogs
Achieve knowledge

My Eyes Laid Upon Thee, Oh Providence

The path I have walked
Dark and deficient in purpose
I could not see
To understand intent
To direct feet
In constructive progress
I was blind
Wandering a void
My own design
It was Providence
That gently touched my arm
And led me to the horizon

The sun did not rise
'Till my eyes
Laid upon thee
Oh Providence

Gentle Persuasions

Creation
Manifests gentle persuasions
Navigates fragile mechanisms
Poise and control
Indicate strength
Inspire humanity
Aspire to be
Like God
Desire to see
Their face
See birds fly
See grass grow
Witness
Amazing things

Man and woman
Create yet another
Tiny little hands
Tiny little feet
Sparkly eyes
Timely smile
Gentle persuasions

Inspire

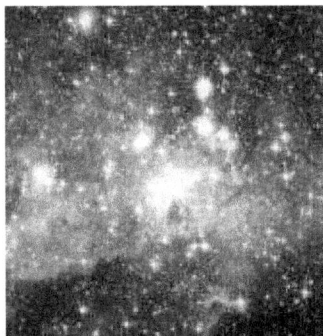

Naught

I understand your words.
I should not be myself?
I don't actually know how to do that.

Non-conformist

In their awkwardness
Words deceive
Know best
By actions
And deeds

Awkwardly Social

Radio operator
The war is over
Troops laid to waste
He continues
Broadcasting
That is his training
His duty
And...
There is nowhere to go

Operator

The Twining (We Are Twine)

Father's Fear
Mother's Pain
Father
Anger and rage
Turn the page
Mother
Ambitious and driven
Father is living
Hardworking practical
Myself disconnected
Lackadaisical

In maturity
Undeniably the same
A product of collective pain
A catalyst of an unknown
        Future
STOP RIP TIME
        Suture

Father's Depression
Mother's Cynicism
To criticism
Meticulous salacious
High form articulation
And I the same
A product and a catalyst
That is the twining

A deadening roar to notoriety
A whisper to anonymity
The whisper falls
    to a soft roar
    to a deadening whisper
    to a sustained gaseous moan
    to a high pristine
    exultant tone
So on and so on
    and so I own
A product and a catalyst of an unknown
    Future
STOP RIP TIME
    Suture
That is the twining

I only hope in life
    to be civil
I hope in death
    to find peace

Craven Minds

The world cried softly
Wary not to be heard
Unseen walls
And desolate space
Witnessed
And were cursed

It wept
For a passing era
Demised by
Poison-medicine
Progress in greed

It wept
Then wailed
Quickly turned
And laughed low
Wary not to be heard
Afraid of unknown things
Locked in ignorance

The world wept
Then wailed
Quickly turned
And laughed low
Wary not to be heard
Afraid of unknown things
Locked in indifference

The world cried softly
Turned and turned
Laughed and laughed
Celebrated unweighted feet
Walked unstable regions
Of craven minds

Imaging In Storm

Skies darken
A storm on the brew
Specks of lightning glisten
In black canvas heavens

Into view she comes
Long silky hair
Color black
Lifts lightly with breeze
Face glows brightly
Surrounding a friendly smile

Only an instant
She looks at him
Her jubilant coal black eyes
Give sparkle
Reflecting a lonely bit of light
Dimly making way
Through active storm clouds

Winds stir
Clouds march
Dark

A precision convocation
Imaging ancient knights'
Victorious return
Lightning flash
And thunder roar
Sounding news
Of comrades lost
Widows crying
Drops of rain
Softly touch his head
Booming loud
In a mournful soul

Harnessed winds
She mounts and soars
He envies her
He stands bewildered
Waiting for a breeze
To come
To lift his spirit high

Shadow

Shadow at the door
Shadow from times before

Do not call its attention
Neither call its name
Choose not make mention of
Nor play its lonesome game

Its silence teaches lessons of
Eternal truth and fallacy
Its presence teaches lessons of
Mortal life and immortality

Leave it be
It leaves be
Ask not where it goes
Ask not what it sees
Heaven or hell below?

See not what it sees
Believe not what it believes
Fire and wind in trees?

When winds blow
Does see evil foes?
When trees bend
Peek beloved friends?

Adhere suggestion
Learn lessons
Truth, fallacy?
Mortality, immortality?

Adhere suggestion
Learn lessons well
So not to be
Shadow at the door
Shadow from times before

Time Has Passed

Moons dominate the sky
Fireflies the land
This night
The ground is wet

The air is wet
Gray-brown marshlands
Black oily swamps
Decay
Defecation
Death
Millions of years
Predators battle
For food
For life

Bones rise high
Through fog
Show their shape
In moons' light
Proof
Their macabre existence
Proof
Time has passed

Shelter Under Foot
(The Wings Of Lucifer)

Beauty and grace intoxicate
Amiable grimace a given
The *affect* is open and disarming

Fallen angels have wings aflame
Opaque plumage impeccably laid
Feathers shown mother-of-pear
Cast a shadow like sunlight
The expansiveness is staggering
In the path of one bound to earth
Indiscernible shapes
For one blind eye turned
One eye rankled with soot

Fallen angels have wings
And great flowing robes
Splendid and brilliant like
Pearls strung across the heavens
Inspiring red clay to take form
Reaching upward
With desire to caress

In a sensual manner
Yet, never in hand
The discouraged become wanton
And fallen angels offer consolation

Shelter under foot
Sanctuary in disillusionment
The promise of honor
In senseless deaths
Not knowing of the trickery

Spiritual Litigations

Light is shadow
Darkness dominions
Little truth
In perverse opinions

All face fears
Stand on trial
Wanton desires
What is vile

All face fears
No rest for the idle
Lose what is dear
What remains is bile

Lethargic time
Spiritual litigations
Apathetic humanity
Trials and tribulations

Perhaps...

Be this
Be that
Perhaps...
Nothing
Perhaps a thought
Perhaps naught
Perhaps insight
Perhaps starlight

Perhaps...
Nothing

Perhaps...

Life

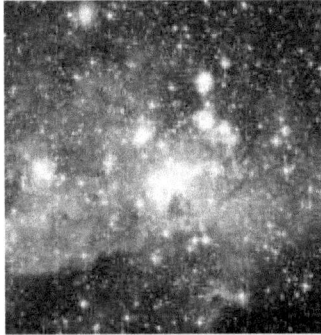

Memes... and posts

/mēm/ noun

elements of behaviors, concepts, or ideas
passed culturally by means of duplication,
imitation, or facsimile

I refuse to use emojis.
When I text, I spell out
"sad face emoji".

Can one be
acutely obtuse?

Everything in the Universe
finds its way to Facebook.
That sock you lost
in the laundry...

Facebook

"Canada? No. I'm going to the North Pole to find the last ice cube."

MOVIE FODDER'S DILEMMA

"I need the work! But why do I have to pet the shark?"

A dolt, a dummy, and a dullard walk into a bar. The bartender says, "You shouldn't drink alone."

A broken clock
is correct twice a day.

A slow clock
is only correct when reset.

My clock
is not broken;
it's just a little off.

"If they have a plastic bat and you don't see a Whiffle Ball, take 'em out."

LEO Roll Call

Guns don't kill people.
People kill people.
That's why people
shouldn't have guns.

Acutely obtuse...

I have a short time to live
Only one death to give
Fight for this cause
Without pause
Neither peace in this land
Nor peace on these shores
'Till the evil of slavery
Is no more

John Brown

Egotism and hubris are the luxuries of small children to be unlearned as we age.

Infinity...

Always one step further than one step taken...
Quality of steps over quantity...
Be a good person.

A riddle
Wrapped
In a mysterious
Black man

Enigma

Humanity may bind my body,
but never my love...
for humanity.

Agápē

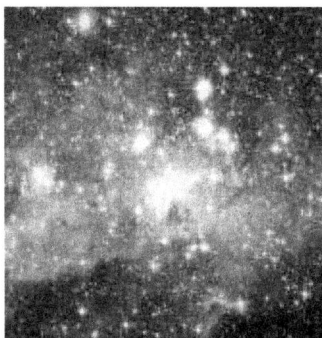

The Holy Mendicant's Brother

Measuring oneself against another,
leads either to envy or arrogance.
Measure one against self,
count blessings, and move forward.

Measure Self

"You mourn the stars? They shine still. You cannot see them, yet they are overhead."

"Daylight is good, but not for stargazing."

"Why do you darken my doorway?"

"Your room has no light. I bring a candle."

"Brother... I dreamt that I was in the path of a great storm. I wanted to run, but could not move away."

"There will always be storms. Run, and you will forever run."

"Brother, some remark that we are
different, you and I."

"Pour water from one cup into another;
the water is the same. Clearly, the cups are
different, but not very…"

"I am not blessed as are you."

"We have great potential. Yet, we resist. We demonstrate cruelty at every turn."

"Brother, why do you say *we*? You are kind."

"I could stand by my house that is untouched by flame, and point, as my neighbor's house burns to ash. I could say that God has shown me favor. To speak as such is sanctimonious. It is not righteous."

'Brother, our well is nearly dry.
What will we do?'

"The nature of water is to flow and move. Rain needs no introduction to the river. They are one and the same. We should do as water does."

"You did not go to the market?"

"There are conditions and contracts.
I have no coin."

"If in my hand a coin, in your hand a
coin... There is no condition. It is the
same coin. It is the same hand."

"I provide you sustenance when you have none. Is that charity? Are we not brothers?"

"It is not charity. We are brothers."

"Brother! There was a good man at the market! I asked how was it, that he was so happy. He told me to find the quickest path to my own happiness. Yet, he did not point in any way."

"There is no way to point. You are a good man. Where you are, it will be. It is not on a mountaintop, waiting. Happiness will be there, when you arrive."

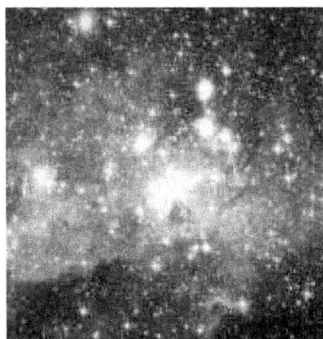

Coda

...thoughtful finale

Je suis Gallus.
Je n'ai pas peur.

(I am Gallus. I am not afraid.)

Not much is truly my own
I observe and interpret
I express best
With images

I crystalize

Poetry Life Crystalized

What truly shines
Will always shine

We are twine

I remember
So not to be forgotten

Dream of spring
In September

Thoughts of heaven
Approach December

Compilation

In the naught
I saw a star fall
And it saw me
Falling...
Falling...

In the morn
The star rose
Faded in light
And it saw me
Fading...
Fading...

Faded in Light

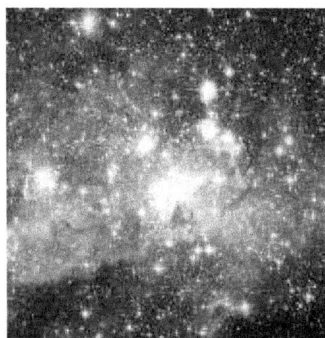

Thank you for reading
Stars at Naught.
Look for a new title in 2018.
Sincerely,

Owen Patterson